INSPIRATIONAL LIVES

TONY HAWK

SKATEBOARDING LEGEND

Clive Gifford

WAYLAND

"The best day of my life"

June 27th, 1999. Tony Hawk was already the most famous skateboarder in the world and a pioneer of **marketing** the sport via video games, books and skateboard gear. He had won every skateboarding competition there was to win but now, in front of a giant crowd of 50,000 spectators at the 1999 X Games in San Francisco, he was about to go further.

TOP TIP

Tony strongly believes that you have to have courage to attempt something you may fail at and the persistence to keep on attempting it until you succeed.

Tony flies through the air as he performs a spectacular routine at the X Games in 1998. The event was held in his home town of San Diego in California.

Skateboarding is performed for fun and the challenge but also competitively at meets called **jams** and contests. Judges award their marks, giving the winning skateboarder the highest marks for the best routine. Tony was taking part in the best trick competition at the X Games with other top skateboarders such as Bucky Lasek and Andy MacDonald. But he wasn't that concerned about winning the competition. Instead, this time, he was competing against himself.

Tony had a list of tough moves that he'd always wanted to master. Over the years, he had ticked them all off, managing to "nail" (perform) extremely hard moves such as the **varial 720** and the **ollie 540**. But one remained – the 900. This is a phenomenally difficult trick: skateboarders fly through the air making two and a half complete turns totalling 900 degrees of rotation before landing safely on their board.

Tony had spent 13 years trying to nail this move without success but that night he felt good and ready to risk failure in front of the 50,000 fans. Eleven times he climbed the ramp, built up speed on his board and took off but just failed to complete the trick. Urged on by his fellow skaters, he launched himself for a twelfth time, span and landed, feet on the board. Yes! Tony had nailed the 900. He described it as, "The best day of my life".

Tony wins the Action Sports Achievement Award trophy at a ceremony run by TV channel ESPN in 2001. He has remained a popular figure with successive generations of young people.

INSPIRATION

Tony was inspired by the attitude of the other skaters at the X Games who applauded his efforts the night he pulled the 900, and wrote in his 2002 **autobiography**, "Skating is not about winning, it's about skating the best you can and mutual appreciation. It's about pulling a trick after years of not being able to and having other skaters be happy for you."

A hyperactive child

Tony was born Anthony Frank Hawk in San Diego, California in May 1968. His parents, Frank and Nancy, already had three older children – Steve who was 12 years old when Tony was born and Lenore and Patricia who were both teenagers and away at college. Tony's father had been in the US Navy and had flown bomber aircraft during World War II and the Korean War. His belief in discipline and order made the behaviour of his youngest child, Tony, a real challenge.

WOW!

Tony once set up his own classroom in his parents' back yard and taught mathematics to some of his schoolfriends. About the same time he was given an IQ test at school and scored 144 which put him in the "gifted" category.

Tony was hyperactive. He was highly energetic but also naughty, frequently bursting into temper tantrums and unable to sit still, stop talking or concentrate. Things got so bad at home that his parents stopped inviting guests round. Going out was little better as Tony would frequently insist on ordering the biggest milkshake, drink it all down and then refuse to eat his meal. At school, Tony was still restless but better behaved. He was very good at certain subjects and at the age of seven was moved up two grades to study maths with nine- and ten-year-old pupils.

Tony poses for a photograph with his parents, Frank and Nancy. They would both support him greatly through his early skateboarding career.

Nancy, Tony's mother, was studying for a college masters degree in education but in her spare time she tried to channel her young son's enormous energy levels into different sports, taking him swimming, teaching him tennis and enrolling him in little league baseball where Tony's father acted as team coach. Tony proved very competitive but couldn't handle losing baseball games. He was still searching for something that suited and inspired him.

Tony's brother Steve had moved away to study journalism at college. During one of his visits home, he went into the garage and pulled out his old skateboard. It was a well-used board made of fibreglass and with a heavily worn **kick tail**. At nine years old Tony struggled to balance on the board and make it turn, but his brother patiently spent the whole day instructing him. Tony didn't know it at the time, but he had found his sport.

Tony acts up for the camera at a visit to a skatepark. He wears wrist guards on his hands to support his hands and lower arms in case of falls which were frequent when he started.

Bitten by the boarding bug

Tony didn't take to skateboarding overnight. The board was just another toy to him at first. But gradually, he began to ride it more and more. A few other kids in his neighbourhood also had skateboards. Tony started to hang out with them after school working out how to balance and cruise on a board up and down the flat streets of his local area.

The Oasis skatepark was around 20 minutes away from Tony's home. He had seen it from the road and watched the skateboarders from a distance, marvelling at how they didn't crash into each other. Tony pestered his father to let him join the skatepark. Membership was expensive though and Tony's parents didn't have that sort of money to spend, but they noticed his interest and wanted to encourage his focus on this one sport. Frank Hawk built his son a small wooden ramp in their garden for Tony and his friends to skate on.

Tony balances his board on a wooden ramp made by his father, Frank, in his garage. Tony's father became his chauffeur driving him from one skatepark to another.

Finally, one summer holiday, Tony made his first visit to Oasis. The skatepark had ramps, huge bowls shaped like empty swimming pools and curved paths known as snake runs. Compared to the flat streets of his neighbourhood, it seemed liked a wonderland. Tony still remembers his first visit vividly, including the horrid smell of the sweaty old elbow and knee pads all the skaters had to wear. He skated the whole day at the park, never tiring or getting bored. He felt at home and content.

From then on, Tony's life suddenly had focus. On Tony's official website, his brother, Steve writes, "When he started getting good at skating it changed his personality. Finally he was doing something that he was satisfied with." Tony became calmer and more easygoing, although he still pestered his parents for as many trips to skateparks as possible. He took on a newspaper round to help pay for day passes to Oasis.

WOW! Tony was so skinny as a child that knee pads just slipped down his leg to his ankle. He had to wear elbow pads on his knees instead.

Steve Hawk (far right) stands next to his brother at Tony's 2006 wedding to Lhotse Merriam in Fiji. Steve would become editor of Surfer magazine and an author as well as a director of Tony's charity, the Tony Hawk Foundation.

Getting good

Tony's trips to the Oasis skatepark grew more and more frequent. He loved the atmosphere there and the attitude of most of the skaters, who treated young beginners like him really well. Physically Tony was thin and bony which meant he did not have the upper body strength to pull some of the moves the other skateboarders were performing. Instead, he began to develop some of his own tricks including pulling an ollie to get into the air and then grabbing the board.

*Tony pulls a **frontside ollie** at the Del Mar Skate Ranch in California. It was at this skatepark that Tony had an epic crash in which his two front teeth were broken in two. Ouch!*

10

Tony was 11 when he took part in his first skateboarding competition, at the Oasis skatepark. Overcome by nerves, he fluffed even the simplest tricks and did poorly. But he was determined to improve and spent all his spare time mastering ever more complicated moves. When he discovered there were other skateparks in his local area he asked his father to take him to them. At the skateparks Tony gained valuable experience watching other skaters perform and learned how to ride the varying surfaces of the different parks. He got into **vert** skateboarding, performing turns and other moves up the steep, almost vertical, slopes of bowls and U-shaped **half pipes**.

It wasn't long before Tony started entering a series of competitions run by the Association of Skatepark Owners (ASPO). He took these events very seriously, drawing a map of the skatepark where the competition was being held and sketching out where and how he would perform certain tricks. He began to do very well and won his age division at the age of 11. Soon afterwards, he was offered a great prize – a place on the official team of Oasis Skatepark. This meant he was able to practise at his local park until 8pm every night free of charge. Awesome!

INSPIRATION

"If there's one thing my parents are masters are, it's encouraging their kids to follow their dreams. [My father] considered it his job to encourage his kids to believe they could accomplish anything, as long as they were willing to put the hard work into it. My mom was just as positive." – Tony in his 2002 book, *Tony Hawk: Professional Skateboarder*.

Tony competes in a National Skateboarding Association competition in 1984.

Turning pro

By the time Tony was twelve, he had a black and white pet cat called Zorro and was learning to play the violin. Apart from these two interests though, his life was all about skateboarding. When he wasn't competing in events, he was practising and working on moves. Tony was winning local competitions regularly and received his first free skateboard, a present from the Dogtown company who became his first **sponsor**.

WOW!

Tony never got the chance to accept the CASL's Most Improved Skater award because as he headed to the ceremony on his skateboard, he hit a crack in the pavement, fell and was concussed.

As Tony became a teenager there was a sudden slump in the popularity of skateboarding as a sport. Skater numbers dropped and ASPO, the organisation that ran many competitions, closed down. Tony's father along with a handful of other adults formed the California Amateur Skateboard League (CASL) in 1980 to allow the remaining **amateur** skateboarders to compete in events. Tony's father then turned his attention to **professional** skateboarding and in 1983 helped organise the National Skateboarding Association, again to run events.

Steve Caballero performs an invert move above a pool bowl during a 1985 National Skateboarding Association competition. Caballero was one of Tony's heroes and the inventor of many tricks still used in skateboarding today.

Tony was fortunate enough to live in California, which at the time was the centre of the skateboarding universe. Many of the great professional skateboarders of the time lived and skated there and Tony had the chance to meet and see them in action. These skaters included Steve Caballero (see page 12) and Mike McGill who were both members of Bones Brigade. This was an exciting and highly talented team run by George Powell and Stacy Peralta. Peralta had been the greatest skateboarder around in the 1970s until he retired after breaking both his arms.

Tony was still just 13 when he was invited to join Bones Brigade to skate as an amateur. He was stunned and couldn't quite believe it. A year later, team boss, Stacy Peralta suggested that Tony should turn professional.

INSPIRATION

Stacy Peralta inspired Tony and helped give him the self-belief to compete against older, professional skaters. In his autobiography, Tony wrote, "My entire career would have been different if Stacy hadn't had the confidence in my skating to pull us both through the rough times."

Tony performs a routine for a photo shoot at night for the famous American magazine Sports Illustrated. "It will be a long time before anyone like him comes along again," stated the article about Tony that accompanied the photos.

High school star

Tony's professional career started shakily. Nervous and a little out of his depth, he performed poorly during his first professional competitions. As he began to improve, he also had to encounter hurtful gossip. Some people suggested that his high scoring was due to his father who remained involved in the National Skateboarding Association. Tony managed to brush these accusations off simply by skating better and better and performing ever more advanced routines until, in 1983, he won the NSA world championship.

HONOURS BOARD

Tony won 73 of the 103 professional competitions he entered. He finished second in a further 19 competitions.

Tony followed up with win after win at competitions all over North America. He made trips to Europe for skateboarding demonstrations (demos) and to Japan to star in a show about talented children.

Tony skates in Vancouver, Canada in 1986 at the NSA World Championships. He went on to win the vert competition at this event.

By the mid-1980s skateboarding was booming in popularity and Tony's skateboards made and sold by Powell Peralta were bestsellers. With other companies such as Stubbies clothes and Mountain Dew soft drink paying him to advertise their products, Tony was becoming a very wealthy teenager, receiving cheques for thousands of dollars each month.

WOW!

Tony's first signature skateboard came with a hawk that he had drawn on the underside of the deck. The design sold just five skateboards for which Tony earned 85 cents (about 60p) per board.

Tony was only 17 when he put much of the money he'd won towards buying a house in Carlsbad, California. He also bought a luxury Lexus car and funded wild parties at his new home. In 1988, Tony and his girlfriend of four years Cindy Dunbar moved into a second house in Fallbrook, California. Tony spent around US$30,000 (£20,000) building a giant 12m wide and 3.5m high skate ramp on the property. Two years later, he and Cindy got married. However, after the peaks of the late 1980s skateboarding was about to enter another trough.

Tony poses with his skateboard during a 1986 photoshoot for Sports Illustrated *magazine.*

Building Birdhouse

In 1991, Tony and Per Welinder, a Swedish skateboarder who had ridden with the Bones Brigade team, formed their own company, Birdhouse Projects. Tony invested most of his savings in the company and the team released a promotional video called *Feasters*. The timing could not have been worse. Within months of the company starting up, a massive slump hit skateboarding, far bigger than the one Tony had encountered as a young teenager.

Sales of Birdhouse boards and accessories began to dry up as did the number of professional competitions and events. Tony, Per and other skateboarders decided to hit the road, travelling to perform demonstrations all over North America. However, crowds were decreasing in size and sometimes **promoters** would simply not pay the performers even after they had skated.

Per Welinder riding for Powell Peralta's Bones Brigade competes in a National Skateboarding Association event in 1984. The following year, Welinder performed skateboarding stunts in the movie **Back to the Future**.

WOW!

Stacy Peralta became a film director and directed some of the action sequences of the movie *Police Academy 4* featuring Tony and other Bones Brigade skaters.

16

Per and Tony discussed giving up Birdhouse many times, but decided to continue. They slashed costs. Tony sold his Fallbrook house with the giant skate ramp, and the five-person Birdhouse skate team crammed inside a small, smelly minivan which they used to tour around the United States. Tony had become a father in 1992 with the birth of Hudson Riley Hawk. But the strain of touring, making little money and fearing for the future led to Tony and Cindy splitting up, although they remained good friends and worked hard together to bring up their young son.

Birdhouse managed to survive and continues to this day as Birdhouse Skateboards. On the team with Tony are friends from the 1980s such as Kevin Staab, **street skateboarding** star Willy Santos, and Shaun White. Tony spotted White as a nine-year-old skateboarder in Carlsbad, California who visited skateparks during the summer and went snowboarding in the winter. Tony **mentored** White who, since turning professional at the age of 17, has won top skateboarding competitions as well as two Olympic gold medals in snowboarding in 2006 and 2010.

Tony sits with his eldest son, Hudson Riley Hawk. Riley is an avid skateboarder who now rides as an amateur with the Birdhouse team.

INSPIRATION

Apart from skateboarding, the only other job Tony felt he would want to do was video editing. When he was short of money, his parents lent him US$8,000 to help him buy editing equipment. They always backed him to succeed.

WOW!

Money on Birdhouse tours was once so tight that Tony used to check in and pay for a single hotel room then smuggle in the other four skateboarders so that the entire team slept five to a room.

Ups and downs

Skateboarding was still in a slump in 1995 when Tony was asked to attend a new event. American television channel ESPN was planning to launch an international competition for extreme sports such as rollerblading and skateboarding. Some of the top skateboarders were wary of the new television event but Tony and many others decided to attend and compete.

The 1995 Extreme Games were held in Newport, Rhode Island. They were a personal success for Tony who finished first in the vert competition and second in the street event. The TV coverage, which was watched by many millions in the United States, also provided a welcome boost to the skateboarding industry. In future years, the event, renamed the X Games, would become the biggest extreme sport event in the world.

Tony and his good friend Andy MacDonald perform an amazing routine in the doubles competition at the 2001 X Games in Philadelphia. The pair won the event.

At the Extreme Games final, Tony waited for the cameras to zoom in on him before mouthing, "Hi, Dad". Tony's father had been diagnosed with untreatable cancer earlier in the year. He had insisted that his son go the Extreme Games. Straight after the competition, Tony spent a few weeks at home with his parents before starting on a month-long tour with Birdhouse. He was reluctant to go as his father was becoming increasingly ill, but Frank Hawk insisted. On tour with Birdhouse, Tony couldn't help but notice how crowd numbers were up and media interest was increasing.

Tony remarried in 1996. He and his new wife, Erin Lee, had two boys, Spencer born in 1999 and Keegan who followed in 2001.

Tony called home frequently, but sadly his father died while Tony was away. When Tony got back, the family held a gathering at Tony's sister Lenore's house. Many skateboarders came to pay their respects to the man who had helped organise so many competitions and promote skateboarding as a sport.

INSPIRATION

Tony is proud that Frank was alive to see him on TV at the first X Games. In his autobiography he wrote of his father, "It still blows me away to think of how much he did for me."

Video game star

Tony had always thought of himself as a computer geek. As soon as he had started earning money as a skateboarder, he had bought the latest computers and gadgets. He had always loved computer games and bought each new games console as it came out. He had even carried a games console in the glove compartment of his car fixed to a screen so that passengers could play while he was driving and he could play when the car was parked.

As computing power increased in the 1990s, Tony began to get excited about the possibility of building a realistic skateboarding computer game which could give players a real feel for the moves and skills of the sport. In 1998, Activision convinced Tony that they could produce a game that captured what it was like to be a top skateboarder and work began.

Tony appears on the set of the TV show Video Game Invasion in California. Tony hosted the show which looked at the rise of video gaming from old arcade games to ultra-realistic modern games.

During the game's creation, Tony had to dress up in what he described as "the worst outfit ever". It was a stretchy, skintight suit covered with white balls like table tennis balls on all his joints, arms and legs. This suit and a series of high-speed cameras captured all his movements as he performed his skateboarding tricks and moves in the studio. With the filming finished, Tony recorded his voice onto the soundtrack. He was sent versions or parts of the game to play so that he could comment on how well it worked and played and whether it was accurate, fun and challenging.

HONOURS BOARD

Tony's video games have been converted for just about every games console available. They have generated sales of over US$2,100 million (about £1,600 million).

WOW!

During his first sessions in the motion capture studio in 1998, Tony thought that the balls on his suit were table tennis balls so wasn't worried when he fell and crushed lots of them...several times. They turned out to cost US$90 (about £60) each.

The first game was surprisingly hard work but very rewarding. Tony Hawk: Pro Skater was released in 1999. It became the bestselling Playstation game that Christmas and was later converted to work on other games consoles including the Nintendo 64 and the Sega Dreamcast. Many sequels followed including Pro Skater 2, 3 and 4, American Wasteland and Downhill Jam for the Nintendo Wii. One of the games, Ride, which came with its own electronic skateboard to ride on, was criticised for poor gameplay, but most received rave reviews and introduced a far wider audience to skateboarding.

Tony concentrates as he plays a skateboarding game with children at a charity fundraising event.

Business booms

Business had already started to improve even before Tony became a video games star. Skateboarding was again on the rise and Tony was swamped with offers of work, appearances and sponsorship. It was becoming a little overwhelming.

Tony asked his sister, Pat, to take charge and help him out. Pat put together a group of people to help Tony, including a publicist to sort out interviews and an agent to negotiate business deals.

Tony's 1999 X Games success when he completed the 900 trick became a big story, one that appealed to people who were not normally interested in skateboarding. This, together with the huge success of the first Tony Hawk: Pro Skater computer games, generated a lot of media and business interest. Tony published his autobiography *Hawk Occupation: Skateboarder* in 2001, dedicating the book to his mother and father. A version of the book aimed at children followed a year later.

WOW!

Hawk Occupation: Skateboarder reached number 18 in the *New York Times* bestsellers list, the first and only time that a book about skateboarding has been such a bestseller.

Tony appears on the popular Jay Leno chat show in the United States to advertise the latest version of his Pro Skater computer game.

Tony's business interests expanded rapidly to include his own clothing company, ranges of shoes and even a Tony Hawk action figure. He was in demand to **endorse** and advertise many different products from computer games to breakfast cereal as well as appearing in interviews on TV and performing demos on tours. In 2002, he set up the hugely successful Boom Boom Huck Jam, a touring festival of extreme sports in which motocross stars, BMX cyclists and skateboarders trade tricks and stunts with each other over a soundtrack of punk, rock, rap and hip-hop played by famous DJs and bands. The tours have been highly successful and continue to this day.

INSPIRATION

Although he retired from competition in 2000, Tony is still inspired by touring and performing jams with other skateboarders. In announcing his 2010 European tour, he said of his team-mates, "I love skating with all of them, and it's like we are a travelling family. They are also amazing athletes and each show is unique because they come up with different tricks and routines each time."

A freestyle motocross rider speeds through the air, performing at the very first Boom Boom Huck Jam. The vert ramp built for the event is believed to have cost US$1 million!

Giving something back

As a famous sportsperson and celebrity, Tony is often asked and often agrees to donate his time, money and spare equipment to help out charities. One of the charities he has supported regularly is the Make-a-Wish Foundation. This gives children who have life-threatening illnesses and conditions a chance to do something they have always dreamed of. In 2002, Tony was honoured by the foundation as its favourite male athlete.

Being a dad highlighted to Tony how important it was for children to have safe, happy places to play. He knew from personal experience how skateparks provided a positive environment for many children who did not fit in elsewhere. In 2002, he formed his own charitable foundation. Its aim was to create good quality skateparks in poorer areas of many US towns and cities which lacked facilities and opportunities for young people.

Tony takes a young boy on his first ride on a skateboard during a charity visit to Cambodia. Tony visited as part of an initiative calling for more help to remove buried landmines which claim many lives in Cambodia every year.

The Tony Hawk Foundation helps people build and refurbish skateparks and also makes **grants** to projects. By the summer of 2010, over US$3.2 million had been given to more than 450 skatepark projects throughout the United States.

In 2006, Tony was one of a group of famous sportspeople who founded a charity called Athletes For Hope. Celebrities such as cycling legend Lance Armstrong, US soccer star Mia Hamm, tennis champion Andre Agassi and **NASCAR** winner Jeff Gordon were with Tony when the charity was launched on national television in 2007. In addition, Tony became a Laureus Sports ambassador, in which role he visits different parts of the world to increase awareness of issues such as fighting poverty or the need to clear buried landmines from Cambodia and other former war torn countries.

Professional BMX biker Mat Hoffman performs an eye-catching routine during the first Standup For Skateparks benefit event in 2004. Tony (far left) has organised such events regularly since, to raise funds for the Tony Hawk Foundation.

TOP TIP

When it comes to campaigning for a skatepark in your area, Tony believes it is important to get as much information as possible on the subject first. "Be involved as much as you can. Go to council meetings, **petition** for funds if you have to, but just be involved."

INSPIRATION

"Who am I inspired by? Anyone willing to take a chance for the sake of progress. I have been inspired by Lance Armstrong a great deal over the years." – Tony Hawk.

A day in the life of Tony Hawk

As a public celebrity, businessman and busy parent, no two days in Tony's hectic life are the same. During a working day, he may have to meet with the staff who run his companies, discuss a new part of a Tony Hawk computer game or clothing line or appear on TV for a charity or to promote a business. On another day he may be flying out to Europe or Japan for a personal appearance or may be on tour, skateboarding and hosting a tour event with additional hours of interviews and autograph signings to perform.

WOW!

In 2009, Tony visited the White House, the official home of US President Barack Obama, for a Father's Day conference. He arrived wearing a suit and tie but had his skateboarding shoes on and later managed to skate down one of the White House corridors!

Tony, Lhotse and their daughter Kadence pose for a photo next to the waxwork model of Tony in action which was created for Madame Tussauds in Hollywood.

When he's not working, Tony loves hanging out with his family and friends, skateboarding for fun, playing computer games, watching movies and listening to music. Tony and Erin split up in 2004 and two years later he married Lhotse Merriam with whom in 2008 he had his fourth child, Kadence Clover Hawk. Spending time with all his children is important to Tony who has to balance a lot of demands on his time. Sometimes he turns down exciting events or opportunities in order to free up time to be with his children.

Tony's current home has two large swimming pools. One is filled with water and features a diving board from which Tony loves to perform somersaults and other acrobatic dives. The other is empty and forms a natural bowl for him to practise skateboarding. Some of Tony's leisure pursuits are as an intense as his skateboarding. For example, he has taken part in thrill-seeking events such as the Gumball 3000 – a 4,800km (3,000 mile) international rally in luxury sports cars.

INSPIRATION

As a famous athlete Tony is an important **role model** for younger skateboarders. He remembers how helpful most professional skateboarders were to him when he was young and always tries to be polite and friendly. In his autobiography he gives this advice: "Become a mentor. Hang with and encourage the people who will inevitably replace you ... find the kids who are doing what you did at that age, and have the humility to let them tell you what's going on."

Tony enjoys other extreme sports including surfing and snowboarding. Here he is surfing in spectacular style in the Pacific Ocean off the coast of California.

The impact of Tony Hawk

Tony Hawk remains the most famous skateboarder on the planet. This is partly down to his superb skateboarding skills. It is also due to the enormous success of his businesses such as the Boom Boom Huck Jam, his computer games and his Birdhouse and Hawk Clothes companies. Tony is the public face of all these products, and this in turn has made him even more famous. Through his work and his success he has helped to introduce and promote skateboarding as a sport to millions.

INSPIRATION

"Tony is the first skateboarder who has given the world a face to put on the sport. He has become a part of American pop culture." – Stacy Peralta, film director of skateboard movie **Dogtown and Z-Boys** and the team boss of Tony's first skate team, 25 years earlier.

Tony receives the Entrepreneur of the Year Award from world-famous boxer, Muhammad Ali in 2006.

From his early days with Birdhouse onwards, Tony showed that in business, like skateboarding, he could learn quickly from mistakes and have the patience and persistence to succeed. In his 2010 book *How Did I Get Here?* he describes how it's important to do something you love and work hard to become the best you can at it. Then, he says, "Once you've achieved proficiency, take your specialty to a level that fellow specialists can appreciate. Innovate. That's what will set you apart."

WOW!

In 2010, Tony went on tour to Europe with spectacular sessions in Berlin, Rome, Barcelona and Brighton. On Brighton beach he performed on the UK's biggest ramp, 4.5 metres high and 15 metres wide.

Since turning 40 years old in May 2008 Tony Hawk has shown no signs of slowing down. He is still skating in demos and shows and still hoping to invent new tricks. He has maintained his love and enthusiasm for his sport and done so alongside being a good father to his four children, and giving other children a better chance in life through his charity work.

At the end of his autobiography for children Tony wrote, "Skating taught me self-discipline at a young age and helped channel my frustrations and turn them into something useful." He echoed this in an interview on the Kidz World website, before another season of Boom Boom Huck Jams, when he marvelled at his life, saying: "I never imagined getting to do what I love for a living and having so many people appreciate it."

In 2010 Tony visited the Indigo Skate Camp in South Africa. The camp is the brainchild of South African skateboarder Dallas Oberholzer who wanted to bring skateboarding to rural regions of the country.

Have you got what it takes to be a pro skateboarder?

1) How often do you ride a skateboard?
a) Every day I can.
b) Some weekends and the odd evening in the summer.
c) Very rarely, I prefer to watch than ride.

2) What do you do if you have a bad fall off your board?
a) Dust myself down and get straight back on my board.
b) Give up for the day but ride again the following week.
c) I don't take risks so I don't crash badly.

3) Are you very competitive when playing sports or games?
a) I hate losing and try to improve so that I don't lose the next time.
b) No one likes losing but I don't give it much thought.
c) It doesn't really bother me.

4) Do you read skateboarding magazines, books and websites regularly?
a) Yes, I really enjoy learning how the pro skaters learn and perform moves.
b) Now and then, but I prefer just to go skateboarding than learn about it.
c) Why would I bother? No one can teach me how to ride.

5) What happens when you cannot perform a trick others can do?
a) It becomes a massive thing in my life. I have to keep practising and practising until I can nail it.
b) I will try it a few times but then let it go and try something else.
c) If I can't do something I tend to lose my temper or give up.

6) Are you prepared to give up much of your social life to devote yourself to practice and competitions?
a) Of course. Pro skateboarding has to become your whole life.
b) I don't mind some practice but want a balance with plenty of time with my mates.
c) No chance. Going out with my friends is what matters to me.

RESULTS

Mostly As:
It sounds like you take your skateboarding really seriously. But are you any good? Start testing yourself out against other skaters at skateparks and local competitions. Learn from the best skaters you meet and invent your own tricks. The sky's the limit!

Mostly Bs:
You really enjoy your skateboarding but may not be cut out for the life of a pro. Don't worry, you can have plenty of challenges, fun and excitement as an amateur.

Mostly Cs:
It doesn't sound like being a pro skateboarder is for you. Perhaps when you are older, you will enjoy skateboarding more and start to think about competing.

Glossary

amateur To do something for fun or the challenge and not to be paid for doing it.

autobiography A book about a person's life written by that person.

concussed To suffer a blow to the head leaving you knocked out or dazed and confused.

deck The board part of a skateboard, usually made of wood, plastics or composite materials, to which the trucks are attached.

endorse To show support for and approve a product in advertising and in public.

grants Awards of money made to projects.

half pipes Large U-shaped structures that vert skateboarders travel up and down, performing aerial tricks.

IQ test One method of testing and measuring intelligence. An Intelligence Quotient (IQ) test attempts to measure a person's pattern recognition, word and number skills and memory.

jam A meeting of skateboarders for a skate session.

kick tail Part of a skateboard deck that angles or slopes upwards.

marketing The part of business which advertises, promotes and sells products to customers.

mentor To help guide and advise someone else, often someone who is younger or who has less experience.

NASCAR The leading form of stock car racing around tracks in North America.

ollie A move in which skateboarders jump up and slide their feet to pull the skateboard up into the air. A **frontside ollie** is an ollie with a half turn (180 degrees) in the air. For an **ollie 540,** a skateboarder performs an ollie and makes 1½ turns in the air.

petition To make a request officially to the authorities, often by letter, which may include the names of people who also wish to make the request.

professional To be paid and make a living from performing as a skateboarder.

promoters People who organise and run skateboarding events, often with the aim of making a profit from the sale of tickets.

role model A successful person in sport or some other field. The way the person behaves is often copied by others, especially young people.

sponsors Companies or very wealthy individuals who provide equipment or money to a skateboarder or skate team.

street skateboarding Skateboarding on streets, curbs, benches and other street furniture.

varial 720 A complicated skateboarding trick in which the rider makes two complete turns (720 degrees) in the air before landing on the board.

vert The type of skateboarding that uses large ramps and half pipes (U-shaped structures) so that skaters perform tricks and moves as they ride a vertical or almost vertical wall.

Index

INSPIRATIONAL LIVES

Contents of new titles in the series